CUTAWAY
FARM MACHINES

JON RICHARDS

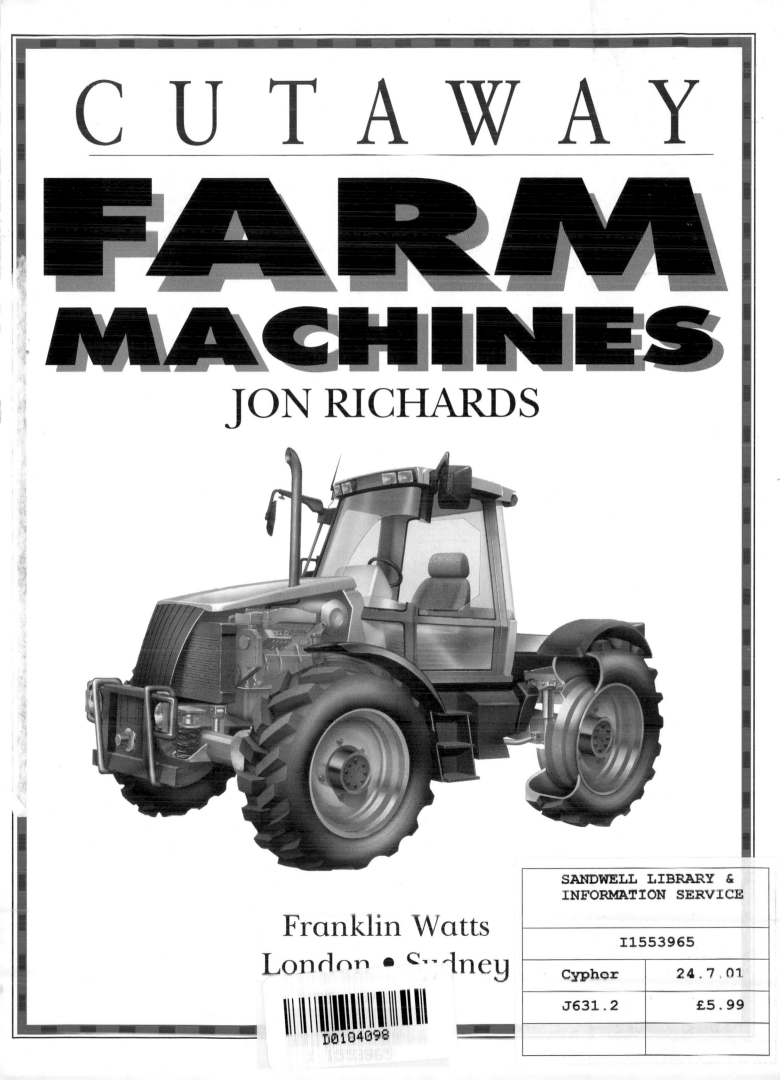

Franklin Watts
London • Sydney

This edition printed in 2001
© Aladdin Books Ltd 1999

Designed and
produced by
Aladdin Books Ltd
28 Percy Street
London W1P 0LD

First published in
Great Britain in 1999 by
Franklin Watts
96 Leonard Street
London EC2A 4XD

ISBN 0 7496 3389 1 (hbk)
ISBN 0 7496 4184 3 (pbk)

A catalogue record
for this book is available from
the British Library.

Printed in the U.A.E.

Editor
Michael Flaherty

Consultant
Steve Allman

Design
David West
Children's Book Design

Designer
Simon Morse
Illustrators
Simon Tegg & Ross Watton

Picture Research
Carlotta Cooper/Brooks Krikler
Research

Jon Richards has written a
number of books for children
on a wide range of subjects.

CONTENTS

Standard tractor 4

Lots of different jobs 6

Changing farm machines 8

Four-wheel drive tractor 10

Massive tractors 12

Preparing the ground 14

Combine harvester 16

Other types of harvester 18

Cotton picker 20

Hay baler 22

Making food for animals 24

Tractor pulling 26

All shapes and sizes 28

Fantastic facts 30

Farming words 31

Index 32

INTRODUCTION

Farming machines have been around for a very long time, helping farmers to grow crops and raise animals. Over the years, these machines have changed greatly, becoming faster and much more powerful. Today, there are a huge number of different machines down on the farm, helping with jobs, from ploughing the earth to harvesting the crops and making food for animals.

STANDARD TRACTOR

Around the farm, the farmer needs a machine that can perform many different roles, from pulling trailers to clearing out milking sheds. The machine that fits this job is the tractor. It can lift and drag heavy objects around the farmyard, and is also tough enough to drive across rugged countryside in all weather conditions. At the same time, the driver's cab is fitted with a tough roll cage. This protects the driver from being crushed if the tractor should tip over.

Countless gears
Tractors have to deal with different surfaces, including dry farmyards and muddy fields. To handle these, tractors have many gears to transmit the power from the engine to the drive shaft and the wheels. Some tractors have 18 forward gears and six reverse gears!

Front wheels
The front wheels of this tractor are much smaller than its rear wheels.

Chunky wheels
The big rear wheels with their chunky tread help the tractor to drive over uneven ground. They also spread the tractor's weight over a larger area. This stops it from squashing the soil, which could harm a growing crop.

Cushion comfort

Some cabs are fitted with seats that are supported on air-filled cushions. These cushions absorb knocks and jolts, giving the farmer a comfortable ride.

Attachment points

Farm machines, such as ploughs and seed drills, are attached to special points on the tractor. The hydraulic linkage can be raised and lowered to hold the machine at the correct height. The power take-off transfers power from the tractor to the machine.

Tractors are used for

Towing a trailer

The simplest job a tractor can do is to tow something – even the smallest tractors are used to pull trailers (*left*). These trailers can contain anything, from harvested crops to manure!

Going up

The front of this tractor (*right*) has been fitted with two powerful hydraulic arms to lift heavy objects. In this case, they are being used to lift and stack round bales of hay (*see* pages 22-23). The other tractor is linked up to a trailer and is waiting to tow the hay bales away.

lots of different jobs.

In the dark

Some jobs on the farm may need to be done at any time – even in the middle of the night! To work in the dark, tractors are fitted with headlights (*right*).

Leaf blowing

Tractors are not only used on farms. This tractor (*below*) is being used on a golf course. It is towing a machine which blows leaves into a pile so that they can be collected later.

Farm machines have

Animal power

Before steam engines were invented, farm machines, such as ploughs, were pulled by animals, including horses and cows (*left*). Animals are still used on farms in many parts of the world today!

Engine power

Although not as powerful as today's tractors, the first petrol-powered tractors (*below right*) changed farming a great deal. They were faster and more powerful than animals, and allowed farmers to work a lot more quickly. The first tractors to use petrol engines were introduced in the 1890s.

changed over time.

All-purpose machine

In the late 1930s, the engineer Harry Ferguson (*left*) invented the hydraulic linkage which joined farm machinery to the tractor. It let the farmer control both tractor and machine from the tractor's seat. The basic design for this is still used today (*see* pages 4-5).

Steam threshing

Some of the earliest farm engines were powered by steam. Here (*above*), a steam engine is powering a threshing machine to separate the grain from the straw.

Cleaner engines

Today's tractor engines need to work very efficiently to help the farmer save money. Efficient engines also give off lower levels of harmful exhaust gases, helping to keep the environment cleaner.

Front attachments

This tractor also has attachment points on its front. This means that a farmer can power and control more than one machine at the same time.

Computer control
Inside the driver's cab is a computer which tells the farmer how the tractor is performing. Because the tractor's wheels might slip in the muddy conditions, the tractor also uses a radar system which can work out the tractor's actual speed!

Rear strength
The back of this tractor can lift a load of over three tonnes – that's about the weight of a fully grown elephant!

FOUR-WHEEL DRIVE TRACTOR

Some of the very latest tractors have four-wheel drive. This means that all four wheels are powered by the engine, instead of just the back two wheels, as in the standard tractor (*see* pages 4-5). Four-wheel drive allows the tractor to find its way over the muddiest terrain. This four-wheel drive tractor also has a special suspension system which allows it to drive on roads at speeds of up to 80 km/h (50 mph) – that's nearly twice as fast as other tractors!

Special suspension
The rear wheels on most tractors are linked by a solid rear axle which has little or no suspension. This means that they cannot absorb bumps in the ground so well. All four wheels on this tractor, however, have independent suspension. This reduces the vibration, allowing it to drive faster on all surfaces.

Some farms need to

Tremendous tractors

This tractor (*below*) needs to be powerful to cope with a huge farm. The largest tractor engines can generate 525 horsepower – almost as much as a Formula One racing car!

use massive tractors.

Monster machines

The largest tractors in the world, such as this one in Canada (*right*), can weigh nearly 24 tonnes, – that's as much as 750 adults!

Double wheels

To stop the heaviest tractors from squashing and damaging the soil, many of them are fitted with double wheels (*below*). These spread the tractor's weight over a greater area.

Machines are used to

Ploughing

Before the farmer can plant a crop, the ground must be prepared. The metal blades of a plough or cultivator are pulled through the ground by a tractor (*right*). These blades break up the soil, making it easier for the farmer to prepare the earth.

Rolling

To prepare the soil even further, a farmer uses a roll (*below left*). Rolls are made up of a number of wide metal rings which are pulled behind a tractor. As the roll moves over the ground, these rings break up any clumps of earth, push any stones into the ground, and squash the soil down to create a good surface for planting.

prepare the ground.

Cultivator

As well as ploughing a field, a farmer can use a cultivator (*left*). Cultivators have a number prongs or blades which are moved through the soil to break it up even more. By breaking up the soil before the crops are planted, cultivators allow more air and water to seep into the earth. This helps the crops to grow.

Seed drill

The farmer plants the crop using a seed drill (*right*). This is made up of a large container which holds the seeds. As the seed drill is pulled along, these seeds are fed along pipes and dropped into small channels which are cut in the earth by small prongs in front of the pipes. The seeds and the channels are then covered with soil by more small prongs at the rear of the seed drill.

Satellite navigation
Some of the most modern
harvesters are fitted with a link to
satellites orbiting the Earth. These
satellites tell the farmer exactly
where the harvester is. From this,
the farmer can work out how much
land he or she has harvested.

Cutting
The large
reel at the
front feeds the
crop onto a
moving, serrated
blade. After the crop
is cut, an auger feeds it
onto the crop elevator
which carries it into the
harvester for threshing.

COMBINE HARVESTER

When it comes to harvesting a crop,
farmers today have machines which can do
the same job that used to take hundreds of

Emptying the load
When the grain tank is full, it is emptied into trucks through this long unloader spout.

Threshing
Inside the harvester is the threshing drum. This has tough metal bars which spin around to beat the crop and separate the grain from the straw and chaff.

Separating the crop
After the threshing drum, the crop passes onto the straw walkers. As the crop moves along these, the grain falls through sieves and is taken to the grain tank at the the top of the harvester. The straw passes up and out of the back of the harvester and the light-weight chaff is blown off the grain using a fan.

farm labourers. Combine harvesters can cut the crop and sort the grain out from the unwanted straw and chaff.

Some of the largest combine harvesters can cut a strip that is 7 m (23 ft) wide – that's as much as four adults lying head to toe.

Cutting maize

Some combine harvesters can be fitted with different types of cutting tools to cut different crops, such as sunflowers. Here (*right*) one is harvesting a crop of maize.

Buried treasure

Many crops grow underground, including sugar beet and potatoes. They need special harvesters to collect them. This machine (*below*) is harvesting sugar beet. It cuts off the green parts of the plants which grow above ground, and then digs the roots out from the earth.

types of harvester.

Picking grapes

Grapes grow on vines. These are climbing plants which farmers set out in rows. A grape harvester (*right*) is a special machine which drives along between the vines, rubbing the grapes off so that they can be used to make wine.

In a paddy

This small harvester (*left*) is used to harvest rice. It has to drive through the flooded rice fields which are called paddies. The harvester has to be small and light to stop its from sinking into the paddies.

Expanding basket
The roof of the
basket in which the
cotton bolls are
collected rises in
stages so that the
picker can hold
more cotton.

Engine power
This cotton picker is fitted
with a powerful engine.
This engine powers the
pickers at the front of the
machine and helps to
squash the cotton bolls
after they've been picked.

COTTON PICKER

Cotton plants produce balls of fluffy
cotton, called cotton bolls. These are spun
out into cotton thread which can be woven

Blowing cotton
Powerful fans at the front blow the picked cotton up through chutes and into the basket.

Automatic steering
This cotton picker is fitted with a special guidance system which steers the machine automatically. This lets the operator concentrate on picking the cotton rather than keeping the picker on course.

Spinning spikes
The pickers at the front of the machine are made up of spiked drums. As these drums spin, the spikes tear the buds of cotton away from the plant.

Up and down
There are special sensors at the front of the cotton picker which can detect changes in ground height. The pickers can then move up and down automatically so that they stay at the correct height. This ensures that they pick as much of the crop as possible.

to make clothes, carpets and blankets. Huge machines called cotton pickers are used to harvest the cotton bolls.

These enormous pickers strip the cotton bolls off the plant and collect them in a huge basket at the back.

Tractor power

The hay baler is pulled by a tractor. The tractor also supplies the power which makes the hay baler work.

Collecting straw

At the front of the hay baler is a pronged drum. As this drum rotates, it picks up the hay or straw from the ground and feeds it into the baler.

Back passage

At the rear of the baler is a ramp. Once the bale is big enough, the rear of the baler is opened and the bale rolls down the ramp and out of the machine.

HAY BALER

After a crop has been harvested, the farmer is left with a field covered with the stems of the cut plants. This is called either

Rollers

The walls of the main chamber inside the baler are lined with rollers. These make sure that the bale is made in a round shape.

Round bale

This baler is making a round bale. Round bales are better at shedding water than square bales. A large, round hay bale can weigh as much as 500 kg (1,100 lbs) – that's as much as seven adults!

hay, which can be used to feed animals, or straw, which is used as bedding for animals. Once the hay or straw has dried properly, the farmer will use a hay baler to collect it into parcels called bales. These bales are either round or square.

Machines are used to

Green crops

Farmers make silage, which is used to feed animals, from green or unripe crops. These green crops can include grass or unripe maize. Here, (*right*) unripe maize is being cut and pulped along with its stalks.

Cutting grass

Here (*left*), a tractor is powering a cutter to chop down grass. As the cutter moves forward, huge blades spin around, cutting the grass. This cut grass is then funnelled into lines called swaths which make it easier to collect. However, before the grass is collected to make silage, the farmer leaves the swaths out for a day or two so that the grass wilts a little. These swaths are then collected using a forage harvester (*see right*).

make food for animals.

Collecting the grass

As the forage harvester moves forward, the spiked drum at the front picks up the swath and feeds it into the machine (*above*). Here, the grass is chopped up finely before it is fed into a waiting trailer and carried off for storage.

Silage clamp

The green crops have to be stored before they turn into silage. They can be stored in large towers called silos, open yards called silage clamps (*left*), or pits. They can also be collected into bales and wrapped in plastic.

Huge engines

The engines used in tractor pulling competitions need to be big. Some of the biggest produce a massive 7,000 horsepower – that's more than 11 times the power produced by a formula one racing car!

Driver

Like all other motor sports, the driver must wear a crash helmet and dress in flame-proof clothing from head to toe.

Little and large

The huge rear wheels give the tractor as much grip as possible. The front wheels are tiny in comparison. They are only used to steer the tractor. Sometimes, they can be lifted clear of the ground.

TRACTOR PULLING

Tractor pulling developed from competitions between farmers to see who had the strongest tractor. Today, it has

Movable weight

During the pull, the weight moves along the sledge, towards the tractor. This has the effect of increasing the weight on the drag plate, making it harder for the tractor to pull the sledge along.

Control cab

At the rear of the sledge sits the sledge's controller. He or she sets the speed at which the weight moves forward, making it harder or easier for the tractor to pull the sledge. There is also a switch which can turn off the tractor's power in case of an emergency.

Drag plate

At the front of the sledge is the drag plate. As the tractor pulls the sledge along, this plate is pushed into the ground until it creates so much friction that the tractor is forced to stop.

become the most powerful motor sport in the world. Tractor drivers compete to see whose tractor can pull a heavy sledge the farthest. Their specially built tractors are fitted with massive engines and enormous rear wheels.

Farm machines come

Tractor on stilts

This tractor (*above*) is raised on specially built axles and suspension. This means that it can raise itself and the spraying equipment above the crop so that any chemicals can be sprayed properly.

Long arm

Sometimes farmers need to pile objects high. To do this, they can use a telescopic handler which has a long, extendible arm (*left*).

in all shapes and sizes.

Tracked tractor

This tractor (*below*) is fitted with Caterpillar tracks. These tracks reduce the pressure on the ground and therefore reduce any damage the tractor may cause to the soil.

Digging drains

The massive claw on the front of this bulldozer (*right*) is sunk into the ground and dragged backward to dig drainage channels. These drainage channels allow water to drain away from a field and stop the soil from getting waterlogged which damages crops.

Fantastic facts

• There are nearly 17 million tractors in the world today.

• The heaviest and most powerful tractor ever built is the Big Bud 525-50. It was built in 1979 and weighs 23.6 tonnes.

• The first, successful, mechanical seed drill was invented in 1701 by an English farmer called Jethro Tull.

• In 1834, an American farmer called Cyrus Hall McCormick invented the first successful harvesting machine.

• In 1837, an American blacksmith called John Deere invented the first steel plough. Earlier iron ploughs got caked in mud, but mud slipped off the new steel plough blades, creating a cleaner furrow in which seeds could be planted.

• Two brothers, John and Hiram Pitts of America, invented a threshing machine in 1838.

• John Froehlich, a blacksmith from Iowa, USA, built the first, successful, petrol-powered farm vehicle in 1892.

Farming words

Bale

A bundle of hay or straw. The largest bales can weigh up to 1,000 kg (2,200 lbs)!

Caterpillar tracks

These are wide belts which are fixed to a vehicle instead of wheels. They spread the weight of the vehicle over a large area and stop it from damaging the soil too much.

Four-wheel drive

This is when all four wheels on a vehicle are powered by the engine. Four-wheel drive vehicles are able to drive over rougher ground than two-wheel drive vehicles.

Silage

Green crops, such as grass or unripe maize, which have been stored for a time in a silo, pit or open yard. After it has fermented, silage is used to feed farm animals.

Suspension

A system of springs and other devices that makes the ride of a vehicle smoother.

Threshing drum

A barred barrel found inside a combine harvester. As this barrel spins, the bars separate a crop into the grain and the unwanted straw.

Index

animals 3, 8, 23, 24, 31

bales 6, 22, 23, 31

Caterpillar tracks 29, 31
combine harvesters 16-17, 18, 31
cotton pickers 20-21
cultivators 14, 15

engines 4, 8, 10, 11, 12, 20, 26, 31

four-wheel drive 10-11, 31

grain 17, 31

harvesters 16, 17, 18, 24, 25, 30
hay 6, 22, 23, 31
hydraulics 5, 6, 9

linkages 5, 9

ploughs 5, 8, 14, 30

rolls 14

seed drills 5, 15, 30
silage 24, 25, 31
silos 25, 31

soil 14, 15, 29
straw 9, 17, 22, 23, 31
suspension 11, 28, 31

threshing 9, 17, 30
tractors 4, 6, 7, 8, 9, 10, 11, 12, 13, 14, 22, 24, 26, 27, 28, 29
trailers 4, 6,

vines 19

wheels 4, 11, 13, 26, 27, 31

PHOTO CREDITS
Abbreviations: t-top, m-middle, b-bottom, r-right, l-left, c-centre.
Pages 4, 6-7, 18t, 22 & 28t – Massey Ferguson Tractors.
6, 7t, 13b & 14 – Renault Agriculture. 7b, 19t & 29b – Charles de Vere. 8 both, 9, 13t – Mike Williams/Media Mechanics.
11, 15t & 25b – JCB Landpower Ltd. 12-13, 14b, 15m, 18b, 24b, 25t & 29m – Peter Hill/Media Mechanics. 16 & 28b – Claas UK.
19b – Spectrum Colour Library. 20 – John Deere. 24t – USDA.
26 – Frank Spooner Pictures.